God's Faithful Promises from A to Z

Artwork by Carolyn Shores Wright

HARVEST HOUSE PUBLISHERS

EUGENE, OREGON

God's Faithful Promises from A to Z

Text Copyright © 2000 Harvest House Publishers
Eugene, Oregon 97402

ISBN 0-7369-0335-6

Artwork designs are reproduced under license from © Arts Uniq'®, Inc., Cookeville, TN and may not be reproduced without permission. For information regarding art prints featured in this book, please contact:

Arts Uniq'
P.O. Box 3085
Cookeville, TN 38502
800-223-5020

Design and production by Garborg Design Works, Minneapolis, Minnesota

Scripture quotations are taken from The Living Bible, Copyright © 1971 owned by assignment by Illinois Bank N.A. (as trustee). Used by permission of Tyndale House Publishers, Inc., Wheaton, Illinois 60189. All rights reserved; from the New American Standard Bible, © 1960, 1962, 1963, 1968, 1971, 1972, 1973, 1975, 1977 by The Lockman Foundation. Used by permission; from the Holy Bible, New International Version®, Copyright © 1973, 1978, 1984 by the International Bible Society. Used by permission of Zondervan Publishing House; from the New King James Version, Copyright © 1979, 1980, 1982 by Thomas Nelson, Inc., Publishers. Used by permission; from The Bible in Today's English Version (Good News Bible), © American Bible Society, 1966, 1971, 1976. Used by permission; from The Promise™ copyright 1995, Thomas Nelson, Inc. Used by permission; from the Holy Bible, New Living Translation, copyright © 1996. Used by permission of Tyndale House Publishers, Inc., Wheaton, Illinois 60189. All rights reserved; from The Holy Bible, New Century Version, copyright ©1987, 1988, 1991 by Word Publishing, Nashville, Tennessee. Used by permission; and from the King James Version of the Bible.

All rights reserved. No portion of this book may be reproduced in any form without the written permission of the Publisher.

Printed in China.

00 01 02 03 04 05 06 07 08 09 / PP / 10 9 8 7 6 5 4 3 2 1

> He has given us
> his very great
> and precious
> promises...
>
> 2 PETER 1:4

Two of the sweetest words you'll ever hear are "I promise." They inspire such confidence! You know you can trust someone when they pledge their honor behind their words and actions.

Our God is a great Promiser. He has given us wonderful words of hope, blessing, and grace in the Bible. These faithful promises remind us of His presence, His comfort, and His unending love. Let these simple verses speak to your heart in any moment when you need a little assurance that He is carefully watching over you and has good plans for your life.

Abundance

I have come that they might have life, and that they might have it more abundantly.

JOHN 10:10

Be glad, O people of Zion, rejoice in the LORD your God, for He has given you the autumn rains in righteousness. He sends you abundant showers, both autumn and spring rains, as before.

JOEL 2:23

He will have compassion according to His abundant lovingkindness.

LAMENTATIONS 3:32

And God is able to make all grace abound to you, that always having all sufficiency in everything, you may have an abundance for every good deed.

2 CORINTHIANS 9:8

Blessing

It is the blessing of the LORD that makes rich, and He adds no sorrow to it.

PROVERBS 10:22

Praise be to the God and Father of our Lord Jesus Christ, who has blessed us in the heavenly realms with every spiritual blessing…

EPHESIANS 1:3

The LORD will send a blessing on your barns and on everything you put your hand to. The LORD your God will bless you in the land he is giving you.

DEUTERONOMY 28:8

He blessed them, every one with the blessing appropriate to him.

GENESIS 49:28

I will bless them that bless thee...

GENESIS 12:3

He who has clean hands and a pure heart…shall receive a blessing from the LORD and righteousness from the God of his salvation.

PSALM 24:4,5

And I will make them…a blessing. And I will cause showers to come down in their season; they will be showers of blessing.

EZEKIEL 34:26

You were called for the very purpose that you might inherit a blessing.

I PETER 3:9

A faithful man will be richly blessed.

PROVERBS 28:20

Comfort

You shall increase my greatness, and comfort me on every side.

PSALM 71:21

As one whom his mother comforts, so I will comfort you.

ISAIAH 66:13

Even when I walk through the darkest valley, I will not be afraid, for you are close beside me. Your rod and staff protect and comfort me.

PSALM 23:4

I have seen his ways, but I will heal him; I will guide him and restore comfort to him.

ISAIAH 57:18

Desires

Delight yourself
in the LORD;
and He will give
you the desires
of your heart.

PSALM 37:4

And the Lord will continually guide you, and satisfy your desire in scorched places, and give strength to your bones; and you will be like a watered garden, and like a spring of water whose waters do not fail.

Isaiah 58:11

You open Your hand and satisfy the desire of every living thing.

Psalm 145:16

He fulfills the desires of those who reverence and trust him.

Psalm 145:19

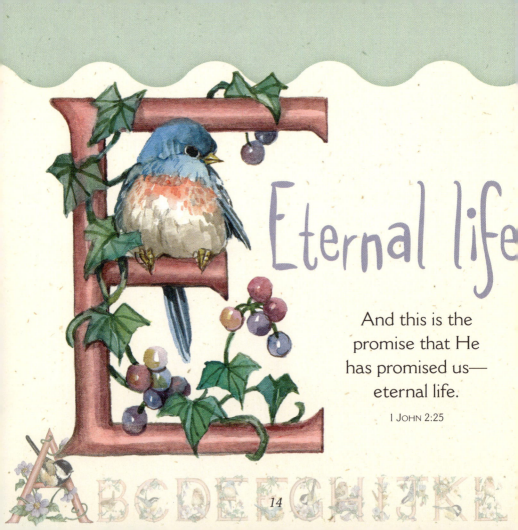

Eternal life

And this is the promise that He has promised us— eternal life.

1 JOHN 2:25

God has also said that He gave us eternal life and that this life comes to us from His Son.

1 JOHN 5:11

Whoever drinks the water that I will give him will never be thirsty again. The water that I will give him will become in him a spring which will provide him with life-giving water and give him eternal life.

JOHN 4:14

The Father loves the Son, and has given all things into His hand. He who believes in the Son has eternal life.

JOHN 3:35,36

My sheep hear My voice, and I know them, and they follow Me; and I give eternal life to them.

JOHN 10:27,28

He who hears My word, and believes Him who sent Me, has eternal life.

JOHN 5:24

And this is eternal life, that they may know You, the only true God, and Jesus Christ whom You have sent.

JOHN 17:3

The gift of God is eternal life in Christ Jesus our Lord.

ROMANS 6:23

Faithful

The Lord is faithful,
and He will strengthen
and protect you...

2 Thessalonians 3:3

God, who has called you into fellowship with his Son Jesus Christ our Lord, is faithful.

1 CORINTHIANS 1:9

Know therefore that the LORD your God is God; he is the faithful God, keeping his covenant of love to a thousand generations of those who love him and keep his commands.

DEUTERONOMY 7:9

And I will rejoice over them to do them good, and I will faithfully plant them in this land with all My heart and with all My soul.

JEREMIAH 32:41

Grace

For the LORD God is a sun and shield; the LORD gives grace and glory; no good thing does He withhold from those who walk uprightly.

PSALM 84:11

He has showered down upon us the richness of His grace—for how well He understands us and knows what is best for us at all times.

EPHESIANS 1:7,8

For of His fulness we have all received, and grace upon grace.

JOHN 1:16

My grace is sufficient for you.

2 CORINTHIANS 12:9

Hope

Be of good courage, and He shall strengthen your heart, all you who hope in the LORD.

PSALM 31:24

The eyes of the Lord are on those... whose hope is in his unfailing love.

PSALM 33:18

O Israel, hope in the LORD; for with the LORD there is unfailing love and an overflowing supply of salvation.

PSALM 130:7

My flesh and my heart may fail, but God is the strength of my heart and my portion forever.

PSALM 73:26

Inheritance

The lines have fallen to me
in pleasant places; yes,
I have a good inheritance.

PSALM 16:6

You will bring them in and plant them in the mountain of Your inheritance, in the place, O Lord, which You have made for Your own dwelling, the sanctuary, O Lord, which Your hands have established.

Exodus 15:17

The Lord knows the days of the blameless; and their inheritance will be forever.

Psalm 37:18

You will show me the path of life; in Your presence is fullness of joy; at Your right hand are pleasures forevermore.

PSALM 16:11

Joy

He will yet fill your mouth with laughter and your lips with shouts of joy.

JOB 8:21

Therefore the redeemed of the LORD shall return, and come with singing unto Zion; and everlasting joy shall be upon their head: they shall obtain gladness and joy; and sorrow and mourning shall flee away.

ISAIAH 51:11

You will go out in joy and be led forth in peace; the mountains and hills will burst into song before you, and all the trees of the field will clap their hands.

ISAIAH 55:12

Keep

And behold, I am with you, and will keep you wherever you go, and will bring you back to this land; for I will not leave you until I have done what I have promised you.

Genesis 28:15

He will not allow your foot to slip; He who keeps you will not slumber…The LORD is your keeper; the LORD is your shade on your right hand.

PSALM 121:3,5

I am not ashamed, for I know whom I have believed and am persuaded that He is able to keep what I have committed to Him until that Day.

2 TIMOTHY 1:12

You will keep in perfect peace all who trust in You, whose thoughts are fixed on You!

ISAIAH 26:3

Love

For God so loved the world, that He gave His only begotten Son, that whoever believes in Him should not perish, but have eternal life.

JOHN 3:16

For I am persuaded that neither death nor life, nor angels nor principalities nor powers, nor things present nor things to come, nor height nor depth, nor any other created thing, shall be able to separate us from the love of God which is in Christ Jesus our Lord.

ROMANS 8:38,39

I have loved you, My people, with an everlasting love. With unfailing love I have drawn you to Myself.

JEREMIAH 31:3

The Lord is gracious and compassionate,

He who loves Me will be loved by my Father, and I too will love him and show Myself to him.

JOHN 14:21

"The mountains and hills may crumble, but my love for you will never end; I will keep forever my promise of peace." So says the Lord who loves you.

ISAIAH 54:10

low to anger and rich in love.

PSALM 145:8

Eye has not seen,
nor ear heard,
nor have
entered into the
heart of man the
things which
God has prepared
for those who
love Him.

1 CORINTHIANS 2:9

God has poured out his love into our hearts by means of the Holy Spirit, who is God's gift to us.

ROMANS 5:5

Mercy

Surely goodness and mercy shall follow me all the days of my life: and I will dwell in the house of the LORD forever.

PSALM 23:6

For it is His boundless mercy that has given us the privilege of being born again, so that we are now members of God's own family.

1 PETER 1:3

You in Your mercy have led forth the people whom You have redeemed; You have guided them in Your strength to Your holy habitation.

EXODUS 15:13

Turn to me and have mercy on me, as you always do to those who love your name.

PSALM 119:132

Near

The LORD is near to all who call upon Him, to all who call upon Him in truth.

PSALM 145:18

You came near when I called you, and you said, "Do not fear."

LAMENTATIONS 3:57

Blessed are those You choose and bring near to live in Your courts! We are filled with the good things of Your house, of Your holy temple.

PSALM 65:4

We give thanks to You, O God, we give thanks! For Your wondrous works declare that Your name is near.

PSALM 75:1

Obey

Now if you will obey Me and keep My covenant, you will be My own special treasure from among all the nations of the earth.

EXODUS 19:5

If they obey and serve him, they will spend the rest of their days in prosperity and their years in contentment.

JOB 36:11

And having been made perfect, He became to all those who obey Him the source of eternal salvation.

HEBREWS 5:9

If you fully obey all of these commands of the Lord your God…He will open to you His wonderful treasury of rain in the heavens, to give you fine crops every season. He will bless everything you do.

DEUTERONOMY 28:12

Peace

I will listen to what God the LORD will say; He promises peace to His people, His saints.

PSALM 85:8

When I lie down, I go to sleep in peace; You alone, O Lord, keep me perfectly safe.

PSALM 4:8

"For the mountains may be removed and the hills may shake, but My lovingkindness will not be removed from you, and My covenant of peace will not be shaken," says the LORD who has compassion on you.

ISAIAH 54:10

Peace I leave with you; my peace I give you. I do not give to you as the world gives. Do not let your hearts be troubled and do not be afraid.

JOHN 14:27

Great peace have those who love Your law, and nothing causes them to stumble.

PSALM 119:165

You will keep him in perfect peace, whose mind is stayed on You, because he trusts in You.

ISAIAH 26:3

For unto us a Child is born, unto us a Son is given; and the government will be upon His shoulder. And His name will be called wonderful, Counselor, Mighty God, everlasting Father, Prince of Peace.

ISAIAH 9:6

*The Lord will give strength
to His people; the Lord
will bless His people with peace.*

Psalm 29:11

He makes peace in your borders; He
satisfies you with the finest of the wheat.

Psalm 147:14

Quiet

He makes me lie down in green pastures; He leads me beside quiet waters.

PSALMS 23:2

He calms the storm, so that its waves are still.
Then they are glad because they are quiet;
so He guides them to their desired haven.

Psalm 107:29,30

The LORD your God is with you, He is mighty to save. He will take great delight in you, He will quiet you with His love, He will rejoice over you with singing.

Zephaniah 3:17

This is what the Sovereign LORD, the Holy One of Israel, says: "In repentance and rest is your salvation, in quietness and trust is your strength."

Isaiah 30:15

Rest

He who dwells in the shelter of the Most High will rest in the shadow of the Almighty.

PSALM 91:1

Come to Me, all of you who are weary and carry heavy burdens, and I will give you rest. Take My yoke upon you. Let Me teach you, because I am humble and gentle, and you will find rest for your souls.

Matthew 11:28,29

Praise be to the LORD, who has given rest to His people Israel just as He promised.

1 Kings 8:56

"I will feed My flock and I will lead them to rest," declares the Lord God.

Ezekiel 34:15

Seek

You will seek me and find me when you seek me with all your heart.

JEREMIAH 29:13

They who seek the LORD shall not be in want of any good thing.

PSALM 34:10

The LORD is
with you
when you are
with Him.
And if you
seek Him, He
will let you
find Him.

2 CHRONICLES 15:2

*But seek first the kingdom of
God and His righteousness,
and all these things shall
be added to you.*

MATTHEW 6:33

The hand of our God is upon all
those for good who seek Him.

EZRA 8:22

Trust

Let the morning bring me word of Your unfailing love, for I have put my trust in You. Show me the way I should go, for to You I lift up my soul.

PSALM 143:8

Commit your way to the Lord, trust also in Him, and He shall bring it to pass.

PSALM 37:5

Trust in the LORD with all your heart and lean not on your own understanding; in all your ways acknowledge Him, and He will make your paths straight.

PROVERBS 3:5,6

Put your trust in the LORD your God, and you will be established.

2 CHRONICLES 20:20

Those who know your name will trust in you, for you, LORD, have never forsaken those who seek you.

PSALM 9:10

Understanding

And we know that the Son of God has come, and has given us understanding, in order that we might know Him who is true, and we are in Him who is true, in His Son Jesus Christ.

1 John 5:20

Then I will give you shepherds after My own heart, who will feed you on knowledge and understanding.

JEREMIAH 3:15

For the LORD gives wisdom; from His mouth come knowledge and understanding.

PROVERBS 2:6

Understanding is a fountain of life to those who have it.

PROVERBS 16:22

With Him are wisdom and strength, He has counsel and understanding.

JOB 12:13

Victory

Sing a new song unto the LORD; He has done wonderful things! By His own power and holy strength He has won the victory.

PSALM 98:1

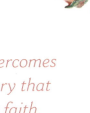

For whatever is born of God overcomes the world. And this is the victory that has overcome the world—our faith.

1 JOHN 5:4

He holds victory in store for the upright, he is a shield to those whose walk is blameless.

PROVERBS 2:7

Thanks be to God, who gives us the victory through our Lord Jesus Christ.

1 CORINTHIANS 15:57

Wisdom

God gives wisdom, knowledge, and joy to those who please Him.

ECCLESIASTES 2:26

Wisdom and knowledge will be the stability of your times.

ISAIAH 33:6

You desire truth in the inward parts, and in the hidden part You will make me to know wisdom.

PSALM 51:6

When wisdom enters your heart, and knowledge is pleasant to your soul, discretion will preserve you; understanding will keep you.

PROVERBS 2:10,11

If any of you lacks wisdom, he should ask God, who gives generously to all without finding fault, and it will be given to him.

JAMES 1:5

eXalt

In Thy name they rejoice all the day, and by Thy righteousness they are exalted. For Thou art the glory of their strength, and by Thy favor our horn is exalted.

PSALM 89:16,17

Wait for the LORD, and keep His way,
and He will exalt you to inherit the land.

PSALM 37:34

Humble yourselves in the presence of the Lord, and He will exalt you.

JAMES 4:10

Whoever humbles himself shall be exalted.

MATTHEW 23:12

He who trusts in the LORD will be exalted.

PROVERBS 29:25

Years

He will not often consider the years of his life, because God keeps him occupied with the gladness of his heart.

ECCLESIASTES 5:20

Bless the LORD, O my soul, and forget none of His benefits; who pardons all your iniquities; who heals all your diseases; who redeems your life from the pit; who crowns you with lovingkindness and compassion; who satisfies your years with good things, so that your youth is renewed like the eagle.

PSALM 103:2-5

The Spirit of the Lord GOD is upon me, because the LORD has anointed me to bring good news to the afflicted; He has sent me to bind up the brokenhearted, to proclaim liberty to captives, and freedom to prisoners; to proclaim the favorable year of the LORD…

ISAIAH 61:1,2

You crown the year with Your goodness, and Your paths drip with abundance.

PSALM 65:11

Zion

They go from strength to strength, till each appears before God in Zion.

PSALM 84:7

Those who trust in the LORD are like Mount Zion, which can never be shaken, never be moved.

PSALM 125:1

How blessed is the man whose strength is in Thee; in whose heart are the highways to Zion!

PSALM 84:5

They will come and sing for joy on Mount Zion and be delighted with My gifts—gifts of grain and wine and olive oil, gifts of sheep and cattle. They will be like a well-watered garden; they will have everything they need.

JEREMIAH 31:12

And I have put My words in your mouth, and have covered you with the shadow of My hand, to establish the heavens, to found the earth, and to say to Zion, "You are My people."

ISAIAH 51:16

The LORD is faithful to all his promises
and loving toward all he has made.

PSALM 145:13